Prayers
Presents
& Pudding

Prayers for Advent
Christmas and New Year

David Gatward

kevin
mayhew

First published in 2002 by
KEVIN MAYHEW LTD
Buxhall, Stowmarket, Suffolk, IP14 3BW
E-mail: info@kevinmayhewltd.com

9 8 7 6 5 4 3 2 1 0

ISBN 1 84003 947 7
Catalogue No. 1500531

Cover design by Angela Selfe
Edited and typeset by Elisabeth Bates
Printed and bound in Great Britain

Contents

Foreword

'Oh, I wish it could be Christmas every day . . .'

'Really?'

'Yeah, why not?'

'You tell me.'

'All those presents, all that great food. Excellent films on TV, lazing about . . .'

'So that's what Christmas is all about, is it?'

'Well, not entirely. There are the January sales to look forward to and . . .'

Ever feel as if that really is all there is to Christmas? That what it's actually all about has been replaced with a glitzy, children's television programme, lots of chocolate, some elaborate shop windows and lots of people asking for what they want and getting it? It's as though somewhere along the way, a bunch of clever people in suits carrying expensive attaché cases decided that what Christmas really needed was an overhaul. It was old-fashioned, tired, worn out. It needed a new look. So it was out with the old and in with the new. And with all that new exciting stuff, there was no room for the real message, no room at all for what Christmas was and is actually about.

No room? Sounds unnervingly familiar, doesn't it? All those years ago, the Christmas story was pushed out into the street, as if the world couldn't quite cope with the unsettling nature of what was actually happening in its own backyard. And it's no different today. The real message, the real Christmas, has been pushed out. There's no room for it any more because we're all too busy trying to work out how to set our video or DVD recorders to record whatever zillion films are on over Christmas, or buying presents no one will use, or filling our cupboards with food that everyone could probably live without . . .

Now think about the characters, about what actually happened and what was going on. Check out the cast list: a baby, a teenage mum, a confused dad, some angels, a few smelly shepherds, some men from the east, a manger, a census, a certain king called Herod . . . Surely this is a story that has more to it than a few drunken renditions of 'On the first day of Christmas . . .'?

The Christmas message is both startlingly simple and earth-shatteringly powerful. It's about God getting his hands dirty, getting involved, getting a bit creative in his approach to trying to get the message of the meaning of life across to his people. And it's about us learning from that, working out what it means to us as individuals and as a family, and then doing something with what we've learned, what we've been given. And, not surprisingly, as Christmas approaches, perhaps our most direct way of getting involved with what's going on, what we see happening around us, is to get in touch with God. It's not a case of us down here and God up there. It's a case of us down here and God next to us, with us, in us. What we need to do is walk with God as Christmas approaches and talk everything through with him, no matter what it is, big or small, important or not.

This isn't a book simply about the big things of Advent. It's not a series of deep and meaningful prayers based on theological ideas and biblical questions. What it is, is a collection of thoughts and prayers about the little things that happen during Advent. It's about how we feel when we put the Christmas tree up, or come home from work and have to go out again to do some Christmas shopping. It's about taking these little bits of our lives, the bits we generally keep to ourselves, and giving them to God. Now that's real prayer.

DAVID GATWARD

What it's really about

Lord,
   I think I might have forgotten
   what this time of year is really about.
It's as if my mind has been clouded,
   silted up
   with muck and grime
   that's peddled as something
   I'm supposed to want in my life,
   to be happy about,
   to desire.

I guess it's easy to get wrapped up
   in the bits that don't matter
   and forget what really happened,
   and why.
It's almost impossible not to get distracted
   by all the decorations,
   the delicious smells,
   the cheesey music.

I think I've become stuck, Lord.
I've become trapped in a world
   full of Advent calendars about pop stars,
   promises of 'two for the price of one',
   New Year bargains
   and TV specials.
It's not a very fulfilling diet, Lord,

and no matter how much of this stuff
I consume,
no matter how much of it
there is in my life,
I still feel hungry,
unsatisfied,
looking for something else,
something really fulfilling.

I want to look
    beyond the adverts on TV.
I want to do more
    than just expect to get
    what I asked for.
I want Christmas this year
    to mean more
    than what I'll find under the tree.
I want to feel the real presence
    this Christmas.

Meet me, Lord,
    on this cold December day.

Amen.

The real meaning

Lord,
  it's that time again.
I've seen it coming for a few weeks now.
All the signs are there,
  on TV,
  in shop windows,
  on crisp packets
  and in newspapers
  and especially in my bank balance.

But the real meaning,
  what it's actually about,
  seems hidden.

There's no evidence left
  of the truth behind the nativity scene
  played out in so many schools,
  in so many department stores.
There's no sense
  of what actually happened,
  what it all really means.
No one seems to be all that bothered
  about why you came to us.

Have we really forgotten, Lord?
Is it really that easy to remove from our minds
  what happened so long ago?

Perhaps it is.
Perhaps it is much easier to forget the reality
    and to replace it with something
    that comes with a 30-day money-back guarantee.

We've created a new message for Christmas.
A message based on fantasy
    and commercialism.
We no longer want to hear what really happened
    but instead prefer the Hollywood approach
    to the Christmas period.
After all,
    why think about a baby born into a cold shed
    by a teenage mum
    and a dad who must have been finding the whole event
    just a little bit difficult to deal with,
    when instead we can so much more easily
    dream of a white Christmas,
    write letters to Santa Claus
    and pretend that in those few days
    we really do wish goodwill to all men?

All those years ago,
    you turned up on our doorstep
    with a mission.
You were here
    to show us what life was really about
    and to teach us that great commandment –
    to love each other as we love ourselves.
A simple lesson

that many of us
still haven't learned.

As I look forward to what Christmas brings, Lord,
    as I try to keep my head above the sea
    of consumer goods,
    festive food
    and bottles of cheap wine,
    help me to see the real meaning behind your birth –
    your love for us.
Your love for me.

Amen.

The glamour of Christmas

Lord,
  I think that sometimes
  I get swept up in the glamour of Christmas
  and forget about the reality
  of what happened,
  the reality of a birth
  of a person
  who came from nowhere
  and infected everywhere
  with his words.

This was a birth that sent shock waves through the world,
  a world that never really recovered.
It was a birth
  that centuries later
  had changed history,
  music,
  art,
  literature,
  philosophy.

This was a birth
  that we've forgotten.
A birth we've replaced
  with a still-life scene of dolls
  in costume
  standing silent

over a model of a crib
holding a nameless child.

What have we done, Lord,
    with what you brought to us?
What have we done
    with why you came?
What have we done
    with the meaning of Christmas?

This year, Lord,
    I want to relearn everything about your birth.
I want to live the words of your story
    and put them into practice.
I want the truth and wonder of what really happened
    to shine through every part of my life.

Infect me, Lord,
    give me some wildness of your love
    in my eyes.

Amen.

A connection

Lord,
    I'm here among friends,
    living my day.
I've talked,
    thought,
    eaten,
    laughed.
I've nattered
    and chatted
    and thought
    and relaxed
    and worried
    and touched.
All these things
    that you also did so long ago.

When I think about it,
    about you living here on earth,
    enjoying other people's company,
    smelling the air on a cold day,
    I feel a connection,
    closer to you,
    like you understand
    what I'm going through.

It's an amazing thought, Lord,
    and one I so often forget.

That you were alive,
that you lived here on earth.
I can look into the night sky
and see the same stars
you saw all those years ago.
I can feel the heat of the same sun,
smell the same sea,
walk the same earth.

At times like that, Lord,
your birth,
your arrival,
makes total sense.
Nothing more needs to be said,
nothing more needs to be explained.
In that moment,
I know what it was about,
why you came to us,
what it means to me now.

Thanks for the clarity, Lord.

Amen.

So ordinary

Lord,
    all that power,
    and yet there you were
    born to this world
    all those years ago
    in circumstances which could so easily
    have been different.

A man
    who learned a trade,
    who grew up in a world
    as real as my own
    and who yet
    still seems to be able to get me to stop,
    and think
    and wonder
    about what life is all about,
    what I'm doing with it,
    where I'm going.

A man who had friends and family.
Who loved them and laughed with them.
Who sang songs,
    danced,
    walked,
    and talked with them.

A man who I don't understand
   and yet occasionally do.
A man who makes me sit and think
   and yet gives me no option at times
   but to want to hide from his face.

A man whose birth
   rocked this world so much
   that all these years on
   I find myself stuffed full with questions
   because of what he did,
   what his friends saw him do,
   the words he said,
   the example he set.

A man so ordinary
   and yet so extraordinary
   that I have no option
   other than to just sit here amazed,
   simply amazed.

Amen.

Wake us up

Lord,
    I sometimes wonder
    if people were more at ease believing in you
    before you actually turned up.
The reality was in many ways
    so different from what they had expected,
    what they wanted.

You didn't arrive in a blaze of glory,
    crowned,
    leading your people.
There was no royal birth
    surrounded by the pomp and circumstance
    you'd expect.
There was no world-wide message
    of your arrival.

You took everyone by surprise, Lord.
None of it made sense.
And today,
    to many,
    it still doesn't.

It's nothing more than a story,
    something that happened long ago,
    something to laugh at,
    joke about,
    ignore.

Now it has more to do
   with children wearing teacloths
   than shepherds visited by angels.
It has more to do
   with what you want
   than what was given.
It has more to do with feeling comfy,
   staying nice and warm,
   feeling safe,
   than with being challenged,
   uncomfortable,
   taking a risk.

We're asleep, Lord,
   hibernating,
   hiding from the message of Christmas,
   happily asleep
   to why you came to us
   that cold night.

Wake us up, Lord.

Amen.

Learning to walk

Lord,
    I think I've just realised
    that all that you are,
    all that you did,
    means a lot more
    than I previously ever thought.
I think,
    against all the odds,
    I've just woken up.

There's nothing more
    that we can be told,
    nothing more to learn,
    nothing more to realise.
This is where it ends
    and yet also
    where it all begins.

You've told us all we need to know,
    given us all we need to live,
    shown us the way
    and now it's down to us
    to follow your lead,
    and trust,
    have faith.

In some ways
    it's a bit like learning to walk.

You watch everyone else doing it.
Then, with a bit of help,
    you learn how to do it yourself.
For a while
    you're helped along the way
    until finally it's down to you,
    and you're suddenly out there
    on your own.

You've shown us how to walk, Lord.
Given us the direction.
You've perhaps even gone one step further
    and shown us how to dance,
    how to jump and run and leap . . .
All we've got to do now is just get on with it.
You'll still help,
    but really
    there's nothing more you can show us.

Be with us, Lord,
    as we take these first few steps
    towards you.

Amen.

My real home

Lord,
    this world spends its time
    looking for something different.
It doesn't want a Saviour who understands us all,
    who preaches 'love one another'
    and mixes with the unloved,
    the unclean.
It wants a Saviour who saves by the sword,
    who smites enemies,
    lays down rules,
    creates kingdoms full of gold,
    ruled by warriors
    brave and true.

But it also wants a Saviour
    who lets us get on with what we're doing,
    doesn't interfere,
    doesn't make us notice
    what's bad about what we are
    and what we do,
    and keeps himself
    to himself.

I live in a world
    that doesn't know what it wants
    but wants what it wants in the same breath.
A world that has had its cake,

eaten it,
and is happy to throw away the wrapper.
A world, Lord,
where often I don't feel that I belong.

For that, Lord,
that sense of not belonging to this,
I blame you.
It's your fault that I don't fit in,
it's down to you that I'm not interested
in what the world seems so keen on.
I blame you
and I thank you,
for that is a world
I don't want to belong to.
A world created by you
that decided to go a different way.

I, Lord,
belong to you
and your vision
for what this world can become.
That is my real home.

Amen.

Dreaming of a white Christmas

Christmas, Lord,
   is a picture postcard.
It's snow on the ground,
   horses pulling sleighs,
   log fires,
   oil lamps
   and parcels wrapped in brown paper.

It's a beautiful scene
   so different from what we see today
   even just outside our door.
It's something we've created
   out of rose-tinted images
   of the way things used to be.

In some ways
   it makes the here and now
   more bearable.
It's easy to forget about today
   if we dream of how it used to be
   and then wish
   it was like that now.
Thing is though,
   was it ever really like that?
I doubt it.

I guess some people
   experienced those kinds of Christmases.

Turned up outside the family house
    pulled on a sleigh.
Then rushed indoors to the fire,
    presented with a nice warm drink,
    as at the piano some ageing relatives
    sang Christmas songs
    to children playing with spinning tops.

But so many didn't,
    and it's no different from now.
We, the lucky ones,
    look forward to a Christmas
    full of more stuffing than the turkey,
    while others wish the season
    would just leave them alone,
    rush by,
    disappear.

We spend this season
    thinking about those close to us,
    the ones who are an essential part of our lives.
But we forget about those
    whose lives
    aren't a part of anyone else's.
Whose existences have been forgotten,
    pushed out into the street,
    told to move on,
    because there's no room.

We celebrate your birth
    and in the same breath

do to others
exactly what was done to you and Mary and Joseph
when you turned up in Bethlehem.

Haven't we learned anything, Lord?
We sit in our comfort,
celebrating,
and forget about those who are freezing to death
on our streets.
The forgotten children of any age
who hope for anything
but a white Christmas.

Christmas, Lord,
is not a picture postcard.
It is a time for us to reassess what we're about,
what we believe,
what we want to do with our lives.
It is a time for us to celebrate our family
and in so doing
get out there and help those
the world has forgotten.

It's not about wishing for a white Christmas.
It is about doing everything we can
to achieve the right Christmas
for all.

Amen.

What I really, really want

Look at this Christmas list, Lord.
Lots of names
    and no idea what to get them.
I've spent the last four hours
    being pushed from one shop to another
    in my endlessly pointless search
    for presents.

I'm tempted to buy nothing at all.
Much better than buying just anything.
But that seems to be what I'm about to do.
Desperation to impress,
    to get something I know they want
    or will like
    has taken over
    from what it's really about –
    the giving
    rather than the getting.

I'm standing here
    obsessed with what my friends and family
    will think
    of what I've bought them,
    whether they'll like it,
    whether they'll think I've spent enough.
It doesn't seem right, Lord,
    because it isn't.

The names on this list
 are everything to me.
I look at them,
 think about them,
 and know that I am rich,
 wealthy beyond anything I could dream.
Yet here I am
 worrying about what they'll think
 of gifts I'm trying to buy for them.

Makes you wonder why I'm bothering,
 doesn't it, Lord?
On the one hand
 I want the presents to mean something
 and on the other
 I want them to impress.
I want the gift to say,
 'I love you this much!'
 and in the same breath,
 'Look how much I spent!'

I sicken myself, Lord.
 I've replaced the joy of giving,
 of showing someone in some small way
 how much I love them,
 with the pain and stupidity
 of worrying about money,
 about trying to impress.

Christmas is all about giving, Lord,
 that's its message.

You given to us,
  to show us a way out of the mess we'd got into.
And also a gift to show us
  how much you love us.
It wasn't an expensive gift,
  it wasn't what we expected,
  but it was given out of love
  and changed our world for ever.

I'm going to go home now, Lord.
I need to think about why I'm out here
  tramping around
  trying to find presents
  that probably don't mean anything.
I need a little bit of time
  to think about the people I love
  and work out a way
  of showing them how much I love them
  without confusing it
  with making sure that the showing
  has an impressive price tag.

Help me remove the price tag
  from my Christmas list, Lord.

Amen.

Lonely this Christmas

I'm lucky, Lord.
I'm surrounded by friends and family.
Some live down the road,
    others are a phone call away.
But they're with me every day
    wherever I go,
    whatever I do.

This Christmas,
    I'll be thinking of them.
Some will be with me,
    others I'll receive a present or a letter from.
It will be a few days of being reminded
    just how blessed I am
    with the friends and family
    that are as important to my life
    as are the breaths I take
    each and every day.

And for once, Lord,
    I do not want to dwell
    on anything other than saying thank you.
So often
    I beat myself up over what is wrong with this world.
About this and that and the other.
About the things I can change
    and the things I can't.

The things I should change
and the things I don't.
And in this state
I forget that prayer
is also about saying thank you.

What point is there to my life
if I spend most of it ignoring the good things I do have
and instead worry about the things I need to change?
I'm lucky, Lord.
I have so much
and I so often forget that.
I become so wrapped up in yet another issue
that I forget just how wonderful,
how amazing,
how exciting,
how blessed my life is.

You have given me so much, Lord,
and with it
I can do even more.

Just now and again though,
I need to stop,
kneel,
reach out to heaven,
and whisper . . .

. . . thank you.

Amen.

Turn off the telly

Right,
 that's it,
 I'm throwing the thing in the dustbin.
There's nothing on
 and I know that
 because I've just wasted half the day
 watching it.

All those hours
 lost to some executive's idea
 about what 'entertainment' really means.
A whole chunk of my day
 washed down a drain
 stuffed full
 with chewing gum for the brain.

I'm appalled with myself, Lord.
This day,
 these 24 hours,
 are a gift,
 something to treasure,
 to use,
 to do something with.
If it all ended tomorrow
 would I really be all that proud
 to look back at today and think,
 'Well, at least I didn't miss that episode of

yet another home improvements show'?
No.
Exactly.

But what's really got to me, Lord,
   is how here, in my own front room,
   each hour has been an open forum
   for sales people to try to persuade me
   that the only way I could possibly ever consider
   celebrating Christmas
   is by buying their own particular goods.

Without them,
   my life is empty.
Without them,
   my table is bare.
Without them . . .
   . . . I'm just a little bit better off.

I need a break,
   a bit of time to reassess
   what I'm doing with what's left of my day
   and what I'm doing with my own particular Christmas.
Have I really got any say in what I do with it any more?
Or is someone else making all the decisions?

Why should I watch this, or that, or the other?
Why should I buy this,
   wear those,
   eat that?

What is going on?
Who gave these people permission
   to come into my life
   and start ordering me around?
And who gave them instructions
   to change Christmas
   to how they think it should look
   or smell or taste?

It makes me angry, Lord.
At Christmas more than any other time of the year
   I begin to see how my life,
   our lives,
   are being run by people
   who spend their time
   happily floating around the Mediterranean
   in a massed flotilla of millionaire yachts,
   drinking gin,
   and trying to work out another way
   to con the rest of us.

I'll admit
   that sometimes that's to do with jealousy.
Why them and not me?
But most of the time
   it's because it's not fair,
   it's unjust,
   it's wrong.

Our world is being transformed.
It is turning into one enormous shopping centre.

The meaning of life
  is now definitely finding a good bargain.
And Christmas?
Just an excuse to buy even more.

What I'm forgetting though, Lord,
  is that I still have that choice.
I still have freedom,
  given by you.
The freedom to ignore the telly,
  switch off from the advertising,
  take a break,
  take a walk,
  and get back on line to what this time of year
  really is about.

Amen.

Santa's list

Remember those days, Lord,
    when I used to write a list to Santa?
    It was one of the major parts of Christmas.
Write down everything you want,
    no matter how stupid,
    then send it floating up the chimney
    because for some reason
    doing that
    meant Santa would definitely get my wish list.

I'm older now,
    and at heart not that different.
I'm the same person
    but with more life experience.
And I still have a wish list,
    but I guess it's changed a bit.
It's longer,
    doesn't have many toys on it,
    and probably has more to do with
    what's good for the world
    than what's good for me.

That sounds a bit self-righteous, Lord,
    but it's not.
I look around me,
    and although I know how good life can be,
    how great this world is,

I also know how much there is
   that needs to change.

I have a wish list
   that probably isn't that different
   from many other people's wish lists.
It uses phrases like 'world peace'
   and 'understanding'.
There's a section on the list
   that asks for an end to famine,
   a world where everyone works together
   for the good of all.

But there's no Santa to send it to
   and no chimney to take it.
I am left only with my prayers
   sent daily to you.
Prayers which do not ask for you to solve our problems
   but to help us solve them,
   to stand with us as we work towards
   getting this world in order
   in the hope that it can really be
   what you created it to be.

Amen.

Putting up the Christmas tree

The lights aren't working,
    there are pine needles all over the floor,
    some tinsel seems to have gone missing
    while in the loft,
    and at least five of the baubles
    are totally crushed.

It's taken me most of the day
    to get this far.
First there was choosing which tree to have
    while trying not to feel sorry for the ones left behind.
Getting that home wasn't much fun –
    it's been raining non-stop
    for the last two days now.
Then once at home
    I had to drag the thing through the house
    trying not to get any mud
    or pine needles
    anywhere on the carpet
    and failing to do both.
Then at long last,
    after much scrabbling around in the loft,
I managed to come up with something
    that looks like a bush
    ravaged by a mad hairdresser
    armed with a chainsaw and some cheap
Christmas decorations.

But, Lord,
  I'm smiling.
Today was a day
  full of the fantasy of Christmas
  and sometimes
  that feels good.
It's easy to become bogged down
  in what's not right with this time of year
  and even easier to let the whole thing fly by
  having not enjoyed any of it.
We forget that this is a time for celebration
  and as such
  requires us to smile,
  laugh,
  and decorate bits of our house
  really rather badly.

So,
  there it is, Lord.
My Christmas tree.
It's not great,
  it's got nothing to do with why you came to earth,
  but it is a visual sign
  that Christmas is an essential part
  of what's going on in my life
  and that it is something
  I want to celebrate.

Amen.

Christingle

At times
   I wish I was still eight years old
   and that holding an orange
   bigger than both my hands,
   gazing at the candle stuck in the middle
   and trying not to eat the currants
   and sultanas
   before the service was over
   was something I could do
   just one more time.

It always takes my breath away, Lord.
There is something deeply symbolic
   about Christingle.
Seeing a church full of candlelight
   and glowing children's faces
   always gives me a sense of hope.

In a world dedicated to being busy,
   the sense of peace
   and of stillness
   takes my breath away.
In a world obsessed with the next best thing,
   with quick-fire entertainment,
   and flashing electronic lights,
   seeing a crowd of people
   stunned silent

by nothing more than a candle
refreshes in me
how great it is
to be a part of this
your creation.

I'm not eight any more, Lord,
   and a Christingle can now almost disappear
   in one of my over-sized hands.
But the wonder of the event
   hasn't left me.
It's simple,
   it's peaceful
   and in the light of the candle
   I get the sense
   that I'm not the only one
   looking to you
   this festive season.

Amen.

Silent night

It's quiet, Lord.
Very quiet.
I've been working hard,
    and now the day's drawing to an end
    and it's time to head off to bed.

I'm stressed, Lord.
It's Christmas and I'm stressed.
Not great really, is it?
This time of year,
    a celebration of your birth,
    of your arrival,
    and I'm tired
    and irritable.

I'm trying to find some good cheer
    for the season.
I'm doing my best to express
    some goodwill to all men,
    but it's proving to be
    just a little bit difficult.

I've got so much on my mind.
Work's busy,
    home's busy.
I've got deadlines to meet,
    presents to buy,

bills to sort out,
cards to send.

My head's in a spin, Lord,
    and I'm desperately in need
    of some of that peace
    I've heard so much about.
I need some stillness,
    some calm,
    a sense of everything just stopping,
    so that I can reassess
    what this season really does mean
    to me.

My favourite carol, Lord,
    is Silent Night.
Something about the tune
    always makes me still.
And the words
    are so apt to how I feel at this very moment.

In this whirlwind
    of presents and pressure,
    I think that's what I need, Lord.
I need some Silent Night.
I need to just sit
    in your presence,
    while all really is calm,
    and just remember
    that on a similar night,

many years ago,
two other people,
under pressure,
tired,
exhausted,
were about to change the world
with an extraordinary birth.

Amen.

The shepherds

Lord,
    I like the shepherds.
They're human,
    real.
They're not people
    with teacloths on their heads,
    forever carrying lambs around under their arms.
They're men who worked a hard life.
A life that probably had others avoiding them
    now and again.

They had hands tough and calloused.
Their skin was wind-dried,
    and their muscles accustomed to long walks
    up steep mountains.
These were people
    who knew dark nights
    of protecting their flock from predators,
    often taking the place of the gate
    at the entrance to the fold.

And these were people,
    rough, smelly, tired,
    who were told in no uncertain terms
    about your birth.

What did Mary and Joseph think
    when these men turned up

to see you?
Were they suspicious?
Were they not all that welcoming?
Or did they just think
    that nothing would ever be a shock again?
And what did the shepherds think?
First angels and now a baby in a shed?

To me,
    the shepherds are vital players in your story.
You were born for people,
    not princes.
And who better than shepherds to welcome you?
These were the first real people
    to come in from the cold and witness your existence.
Real people with real lives
    there in front of you
    as you, unaware,
    screamed into the night.

Sometimes, Lord,
    your story takes me by the scruff of the neck,
    looks me in the eye,
    and says quite simply,
    'You're a part of this, too.'

Amen.

A long walk home

What was it like, Lord?
For Mary and Joseph?
You on the way
   and then they've got to walk
   for mile upon mile
   just to satisfy
   some paperwork.

Not the best of situations, really.
Generally, people take it easy
   with a baby on the way.
Lots of rest,
   lots of planning for the future.
Perhaps a bit of decorating
   in the room that'll soon be holding
   a tiny person.
Somewhat different, isn't it?

The whole situation must have seemed bizarre from the start.
First there's the fact that you're God's Son.
Then there's all the business with angel visitations.
And to top it all off
   they've got to get to Joseph's birthplace
   just at that time
   when your birth is only days away.

Looking at it, Lord,
it's as if you were exiled from the beginning,

destined to live a life
on the road.
Was this really a sign of things to come?

I'd love to know how Joseph and Mary felt
as they walked those roads.
What did they say to each other?
How did they keep each other going?
How did they deal with the news
about who
and what
you were?

They were just normal people
chosen for an extraordinary road.
A road they started travelling
on their way to Joseph's home.

It was a long journey, Lord,
and it didn't end there
when you reached the stable.
It was just the beginning
of a life
that would soon see tired feet
as a part of every day.
A life
that would move from village to town,
never really resting.
A life
desperate to let people know

what life really was about
no matter what the risk.
A life lived,
   a life given.

And it is that life
   that I aspire to, Lord.
I look at you and how you lived,
   what you said,
   what you taught,
   and I want some of that in my own life.

My own life is a journey
   and I have no idea when it will end.
I just know where I am
   and where I've come from.
That's it.
And the only way I want to face my future,
   to travel my own long walk back home,
   is with you.

Walk with me on the road, Lord.

Amen.

No room

At this point, Lord,
   I can well imagine how Joseph and Mary must have felt.
I can also imagine just how Joseph
   probably wanted to react,
    if I think how I would have reacted.

I wonder if by now
   they were beginning to think that the whole thing
   was a mistake?
After all, with the Son of God soon to arrive,
   born by Mary,
   they would have probably expected
   at least somewhere warm and comfortable
   to go through the birth.
But no.
Instead they are pushed out,
   and the birth happens in nothing more
   than a shed or a cave.

What kind of birth
   is this for a Messiah?
Doesn't seem to make much sense.
The Son of God born in with the animals?
Outcast from the comfort
   of being with other people?

But then I can't help but wonder
   if this was all a part

of the over-riding message
of your birth.
From the very beginning
 you were one of the outcasts,
 able to communicate and to understand
 what such people went through,
 how they felt,
 what their lives were like.
A prince among paupers.

Had you come to us
 to thrones of gold,
 would your message have been the same?
No.
Instead you came to be with us,
 to live with us.
To walk with us and to laugh
 and cry
 and hope
 and love with us.

To a world you came that had no room
 and yet you made room for all.
Even me.

Amen.

Wise men

OK, Lord,
   so there is some symbolism
   behind the gifts brought by the wise men.
But I'm not interested in that at this moment.

These were men
   who searched the stars
   for answers to questions.
Not the most sensible of activities
   as far as I'm concerned.
At no point do I consider where Mars is
   in relation to Jupiter
   to have any significance
   on what I do today
   or tomorrow.
Generalisations
   and newspaper gurus
   really don't direct my life.

But these men must have taken the whole thing
   very seriously.
They see a star.
Something so unusual
   that they look at each other
   and go, 'Wow! Check that out!
That's amazing! What say we follow it?'
And so they do.

They leave their homeland
   and set off on a journey
   and end up in a stable
   looking at you
   and presenting you with gifts.

This, Lord,
   is another of those 'here for everyone' moments.
These were men who probably hadn't the faintest idea
   about who or what you could be
   until they saw you.
But they were led to you by a star.
These people from another land,
   standing there at your side
   with Mary and Joseph.

I often wonder how that experience
   changed their lives.
What did they do
   once they'd seen you?
What did they take with them
   back to their homes?
Did they tell people about the baby in a manger?
Did they end their search for answers among the stars
   because there, in that moment,
   their answer had been found?

Like with so much of the Bible, Lord,
   there are so many loose threads.
Bits of stories I want to know about,
   bits I never will.

Bits I don't understand,
and bits which stun me by their simplicity.

Here, Lord,
I'm left wondering about these men.
Who they were,
what they were about,
what they felt when they saw you.
Did you answer all their questions, Lord,
when they saw you,
or like so many of us,
did they go away with even more questions needing answers?

All I do know
is that in that moment,
in your birth,
you had both rich and poor
by your side.
You had people from far away
and those close to home.
And you were also with
the animals of creation.

I may not be that wise myself, Lord,
but I do know
that in that moment,
when you arrived in the world,
you turned everything on its head.
So much so that even stars foretold your arrival.

Amen.

Just a baby

A baby, Lord,
   is amazing.
Every time I see one
   I'm amazed.
I look at them
   and try to imagine what the adult version
   will be like,
   what they'll look like,
   what they'll do with their lives.

Perhaps that's why parenthood is so amazing.
You give life to someone,
   and then you get the chance
   to help them to grow,
   to find out about the world
   and their place in it.
To give them advice,
   pick them up,
   walk with them,
   talk with them.

How did Joseph and Mary feel
   when they saw you eye-to-eye?
This baby, their baby,
   the Son of God?
What a responsibility.
After all,
   it was up to them to bring you up,

to teach you,
to watch you grow.
Even disciplining you
    was their responsibility,
    because I doubt very much
    that you never got into trouble!

They were your parents, Lord,
    and yet they weren't.
Did that thought ever leave them?
Did they ever find themselves
    wondering what they'd let themselves become a part of?

Did they ever wonder about what would happen
    when you hit adulthood?
Did they ever feel afraid for you, for themselves?

So many questions, Lord,
    all from a single birth.
A birth so utterly unconventional
    that sometimes I wonder
    if it ever really happened the way it's told.
A birth of a son
    to two very human people
    chosen by God
    to be your parents.
Two very human
    and two very special,
    amazing, people.

Amen.

As a family

What was your family life like, Lord?
I guess my only frame of reference
   is my own family life,
   and the family lives of friends.
Was yours any similar?

When you were a toddler
   did you get caught
   eating buckets of mud?
When you ate your food
   did you get as much on the floor
   as you did in your mouth?
Did you get excited when you saw birds
   swimming on the water?

When you were ten
   did you go off on adventures?
Did you have a gang of friends
   to run around with?
Did you all have nicknames?
Did you invent your own games
   and play them till you were exhausted?

What was it like when you were a teenager?
Did you drive your parents up the wall
   with mood swings?
Were hormones racing
   through your veins?

Did you spend days
   wondering if there was any point to life?

These are questions
   that will never be answered
   but that I can't help asking.
Sometimes, just imagining what your life was like
   helps me relate to you a little bit easier.
Thoughts of you with your parents,
   just living through the days,
   laughing, chatting.
It makes your message,
   your life
   seem so much more relevant
   and real.

You, Lord,
   had a family.
You lived a life like so many of us
   and yet lived a life so different
   that it changed the world.
From such humble beginnings,
   you gave the world wisdom,
   truth, meaning.
There was no special education,
   no wealth or fortune or favour.
You lived and grew as your people
   then showed them a way
   to really live as a family.

Amen.

Just for the children?

Christmas, Lord,
   seems to be about nothing more
   than making children smile.
It's about buying them presents,
   giving them parties,
   watching them in the nativity play.

It's about Santa Claus
   and more cartoons on telly
   and making decorations at school.

We seem to have given Christmas
   a candy-flavoured coating.
We've taken away its meaning,
   smoothed down its rough edges
   and made it easier to swallow.
And now, so often,
   it seems to be
   nothing more than a made-up story.
Something created
   to make children smile.

But that's not right, Lord.
The reality of your birth is so different,
   so much more real.
Why do we protect ourselves
   from what actually happened?

What is it about you,
  about your birth,
  that scares us?
What are we afraid of?

This season is not for the children
  in the same way that it is not for adults.
It is for us all.
It's time we threw away the decorations
  and got down on our knees in that stable
  to witness your birth again.
A birth to exhausted parents
  in a room smelling of animals.
A baby laid out on animal feed.
Some scruffy shepherds turning up
  with tales of angels.
Wise men from the east coming with gifts.
We've taken your birth,
  given it a good clean,
  and repackaged it to make it more acceptable.
But if there's one thing about your whole life, Lord,
  it's that at no point was it ever acceptable.

You came with a message
  that was rejected.
People turned on you,
  and in the end killed you.
That's just how acceptable you were.

The reality of your birth
  is hard to deal with.

It's so much easier
 if we pretend it's just a children's story.
The reality though
 is something that affects us all.
This is a birth for nations.
A birth for the people of the world.
A birth that stares us in the face
 and says, 'This is where it began.'

Help me get back to the beginning, Lord,
 see for myself
 the reality
 of your birth.

Amen.

Beyond the front door

It's really hit me today, Lord.
The challenge of your birth,
  what it really means.

I have to get out of this chair,
  go through my front door
  and get out into the world,
  taking your story with me.

I have to leave behind what I used to be,
  and with what I now am,
  walk in faith.

It's so easily said
  and not so easily done.
I don't really want to.
It's safe here,
  comfy.
I'm happy,
  relaxed.
Not much is really bothering me,
  life is just pottering along.
But what you're saying to me,
  through your unusual birth,
  is that if I really want to live,
  really want to make my life mean something,
  I have to take risks.

You were born
    right smack bang in the middle of a world going crazy.
You were born to the people on the bottom rung,
    whose lives were hard,
    harsh,
    unforgiving,
    but filled with hope.
And those you met,
    even at the moment of your birth,
    found themselves leaving behind the old
    and going on to something new.

Maybe this Christmas
    will see a new me born.
In the coldness of my life,
    where there isn't much room for anything,
    perhaps I will allow a new birth
    to take me from where I am
    into the beyond.
Perhaps that's what this Christmas is about –
    new birth
    in me.

Amen.

New birth

A new me, Lord,
  that's what I'm after.
Behind all the tinsel of my life,
  the decorations
  and the false celebration and happiness,
  what I'm really after is a new me,
  a new birth.

I want to have the courage
  to stand by what is so easy for me to believe
  when I'm alone with you.
I want to be able to say
  what I believe,
  why I believe it,
  rather than running away
  or pretending I'm someone else.

In my own small way
  I'm a bit like the inn.
No room for you, Jesus,
  well, certainly not at the moment.
I mean, what would my friends say?
What would the next-door neighbours say?
I've got my reputation to think about.

Stupid, isn't it?
I'm more worried about what people will think of me

than about how I really feel inside.
Not very brave,
   not very clever,
   but very me most days of my life.

But in other ways, Lord,
   I'm a bit like the stable.
Unsuspecting,
   unsuitable,
   a bit smelly and untidy.
Hardly the place
   for a Messiah to be born.
Yet that is where you want to be,
   and through my rocky,
   faltering faith,
   that is where I hope you are.

I'm not perfect,
   I'm not anything other than what I am,
   yet, Lord,
   I ask you to be with me
   in my own
   new birth.

Amen.

Proclamation

Each year
 we celebrate you being born to us
 here on earth.
We sing songs about it,
 have terrible nativity plays showing it.
We give presents
 and do our best to enjoy the season of good cheer.
But do we do anything
 with what the message is about?
Proclaiming the good news
 that there is a meaning to our lives?
That we can have an intimate relationship
 with our creator?
That, with effort and work,
 we can make our lives mean something?

Our lives are so much more
 than what we, most of the time, make of them.
They are gifts beyond measure.
A chance to explore and discover,
 to develop and learn and grow.
To get involved with the world around us,
 to care for it,
 manage it,
 get involved with it.

Are we simply afraid to get our hands dirty?
If so,

then we're nothing more than armchair gardeners.
We sit,
  we dream,
  we go to sleep,
  when it is so much more rewarding to get out into the world,
  to smell the earth on our hands
  and taste the sweetness of the air.

So often,
  when we do decide to do something about it,
  we make it all sound so bland.
We happily declare, 'Jesus is Lord!'
  and then leave it at that.
No explanation,
  no rooting it in everyday life.
It's no wonder people are put off.

Following you
  isn't about being happy and smiley all the time.
It's not about walking up to people on the street
    and proclaiming that the good news is here,
    and then leaving them to flounder.

No,
  following you
  is about proclaiming the good news
  that you are here,
  born to us,
  into our world,
  to live with us as we live in this world.

And following you
   is about getting involved with life,
   really living it.
That's the good news.
That's what your birth is about.
Proclaiming that you came to give us life
   so that we may live it to the full.

How, Lord,
   if we shout about it like that,
   can anyone fail to take notice,
   this Christmas?

Amen.

New life

Birth,
   new life,
   is amazing.
We see it everywhere, Lord,
   and often ignore it.
The seasons we live through,
   the days that come and go.
Every part of our lives
   gives us a taste of birth,
   of new life.

I've never been much of a gardener, Lord.
Perhaps because I've never had much of a garden.
But also because I'm not only lazy
   but scared of what could all too easily
   go wrong.
Last spring, though,
   I managed to get a few pots,
   some young herb plants,
   and grow them.
It was an odd moment.
I hadn't really got a clue about what I was doing,
   even though I'd read about it
   and watched plenty of TV programmes about it.
But as I got my hands into the compost,
   put those plants into their pots
   and watered them in,

I felt as though I'd really achieved something.
Not much,
    but something.

Those plants
    were surviving because of the care I was giving them.
I was a part of their growth,
    their ability to survive.
Without me,
    without the water and nutrients
    I had to provide,
    they'd die.

I'll admit that along the way
    some didn't fare too well,
    but most of them grew and before long
    those herbs were not only flourishing
    but even adding a bit of flavour to my attempts at cooking.
I had taken a little bit of responsibility for new life.

And I guess I'm no different from one of those plants.
I'm still in the early stages of my life,
    fighting to survive the seasons,
    but unless I'm fed and watered properly
    I haven't got a chance.
It's easy for me to think that three square meals a day
    will keep me going
    but I can't help feeling that without some other sort of food
    I'll never really bear any fruit.
I need some spiritual fertiliser

to really get going.
Which is where you come in.

Without you, Lord,
   I can't grow,
   I can't begin to realise the potential locked up in my own life.
I have to learn from you,
   be fed by your wisdom,
   watered by your words,
   bathed in your light.
Only then can I really experience true growth,
   new life.

Keep me well watered, Lord,
   and watch over me as I grow.

Amen.

No more pudding

I'm stuffed, Lord,
    I just can't eat any more.
I feel as though I've been eating all day.
Perhaps I have.
That is what Christmas is about, to some degree.
Good food,
    good company,
        and lots and lots of both.

I guess I've gorged a bit on both, though.
But then again, why not?
It's not like we do this every day, is it?

Sometimes,
    when we're sitting here enjoying so much
    on this day,
    it's easy to feel guilty,
    to feel dreadful because we have so much
    and are so lucky.
It's fair enough I guess.
But today, Lord,
    in this moment,
        I don't want to do that.
I want to look around me
    and to say thank you for all that I have.
I want you to know
    that, as I sit here

eating this food,
drinking this wine,
laughing with friends and family,
I am grateful
and that I thank you for all that I have.

I am lucky, Lord.
I am so lucky and sometimes I forget that.
I have so much,
   and I have this life in which to experience and enjoy it all
   and all I can do is offer you that life and all that it is
   in return for your generosity.

Thank you, Lord,
   for all that I have this Christmas.

Amen.

Real smiles, real people

Sometimes, Lord,
    even though it must be easy to look at this world
    and despair,
    you must find yourself just looking
    and smiling.

We're not a bad bunch, really,
    and when for a moment
    we enjoy each other's company,
    celebrate the goodness of life,
    I hope we do give you something to smile about.

This season is all about that.
About celebration and happiness
    and laughter and togetherness.
It's about enjoying the company of others,
    making them feel good about themselves,
    giving gifts
    as an expression of love.
And all in the full celebration
    of your birth.

It's amazing really, Lord,
    that to celebrate your birth
    we give each other gifts.
It's almost a way of continuing the giving.
You gave to us

and in some small way
we give to each other
as a sign of the bond of love
between us
and with you.

It's easy to forget
how important the giving is,
rather than the receiving.
But when you're with real people,
and you see on their faces
real smiles,
it's like a glimpse of heaven,
a quick look at what life on this world,
with you,
really is all about.

You're interested in us, Lord,
the real people
with real lives
and real existences.
You want to get fully involved
in the ups and downs of what we do
each and every day.
You want to kneel with us,
walk with us,
hold us
and laugh with us.

Sitting here,
looking at the faces of the ones I love,

thinking of the others that aren't here,
I thank you for us,
your real people
who you came to all those years ago.
And I hope, Lord,
  that these smiles on our faces,
  this laughter in the air,
  is praise enough to you
  who wanted us to know
  and to experience
  what real life was about.

Amen.

Friends and family

As Christmas draws near, Lord,
   my mind is full of the faces
   of my family and friends.
Some I haven't seen for months
   and others I know I'll be seeing all too soon.

We're in touch by phone,
   by email, by letter.
The occasional visit through the year
   for parties or just to get together
   helps to remind us what we look like,
   what we really are about.
A three-dimensional memory
   of the face behind the voice.

Yet this time of year brings something new
   to the relationships I have
   with those I depend on
   and hold close.
Each Christmas
   means another year has passed.
Not just in my life
   but the lives of those around me.
We can look back and see how we've changed,
   what we've achieved,
   what difficulties we've survived.

And we can look ahead to the next twelve months
and wonder what they too hold in store.

It's a great thing, Lord,
growing with friends and family.
If it were just my life
it would seem so pointless,
but to have so many lives
all growing together
gives a sense of worth,
a sense of belonging,
to everything that I do.

This Christmas, Lord,
help me to remember all my friends and family.
On my own lonely roads
they've helped me survive,
pulled me through,
and in my own small way,
I hope I've helped them.

These lives we lead are bound to each other
and all I can do is pray
that you, Lord,
will help to keep those bonds strong.

Hold us together, Lord,
and if we do begin to fall apart,
help us to retie those bonds
and make them even stronger.

Amen.

Not what I wanted

This is a bad feeling, Lord,
  a very bad feeling.
I'm trying to pretend I'm happy
  with a present I've been given.
And I'm not.
It's rubbish.

Am I ungrateful?
I guess so.
But I can't help it
  if I don't like it, can I?
If it's the thought that counts
  then I can see right here
  that even that is missing.

This is a present bought because
  something had to be bought
  rather than given.
This doesn't say,
  'Happy Christmas!'
  but, 'Oh, well, here you go. This'll have to do.'

Is this what Christmas is getting like, Lord?
A case of, 'Oh, well, it'll have to do'?
Because I don't think it will.
Not one bit.
This isn't a time for putting up with the average
  or the norm.

And it's not a time for just doing something
    because it's just something you do.
No, this is a time for doing something extraordinary.
For getting up and making the days count for something.
For letting people really know how we feel.
Not just those who are close to us,
    but those people out there.
Those people who look at the church
    and see it as nothing more than a building
    full of people
    who've cut themselves off from the world.

Today, Lord,
    we seem to turn to the world and say,
    'Here you go, this'll have to do.'
That's wrong,
So very wrong.
What we should be saying is,
    'Look!
    Look at this!
    And here, let me give you a hand as well!'
We should be getting excited about giving
    not just presents to each other
    but your presence to others.
We should be out there
    unwrapping your birth
    for the world to see.

Tear away the wrapping paper, Lord.

Amen.

So long ago

I feel a bit like Scrooge at the moment.
Every day I seem to meet one of the ghosts of Christmas.

The Ghost of Christmas past
   has disappeared for the moment.
But all he managed to do
   was make me feel a bit rubbish,
   with memories of how Christmas used to be.
I was younger then
   and always got so excited.
Dragging Mum and Dad out of bed
   to open the presents in our stockings
   then a whole day dedicated
   to going crazy
   over boxes of toys.
It was fantastic.

At the moment
   I'm being particularly bothered
   by the Ghost of Christmas present.
And boy is he getting on my nerves.
He's a bit of a party animal
   and very demanding.
Always asking me to get ready for this,
   buy that,
   do this,
   do the other.

I've got a list of stuff to do that's so long
    I can't remember where it started
    or where it finishes.

Now I'm dreading the ghost of Christmas future.
Not only does he look scary
    all dressed up in shadows,
    but it's that sense of uncertainty
    that's getting to me.
Will it all be OK?
What if no one likes what I've got them?
What about next year?
What will it be like in ten years' time?
And what about this and that and the other?

Lord,
    I need a little bit of exorcism.
These fictitious ghosts
    are taking up so much of my time
    that the real reason for the season
    is being pushed out.
I haven't got time to think about you
    because I'm thinking of so much else,
    and the ghosts keep reminding me of that.

What I really need, Lord,
    is to think about the real Christmas
    of the past, present,
    and future.
    the Christmas of your birth

all those years ago.
The Christmas of your existence now with us,
    as you promised to be with us always.
And the Christmas of tomorrow,
    with all the potential I see for your vision
    for this world.

I don't want to dwell on the ghosts of Christmas, Lord,
    but on the real and unconditional love
    you brought to us
    so many years ago,
    that's with us now
    and for ever.

Amen.

Too much shopping

A short prayer, Lord.
My feet are tired
   and my hands cut to ribbons
   by all these plastic bags.

My wallet feels lighter,
   but that's not a good thing at all,
   because for the life of me
   I can't quite remember
   what I've spent all my money on.

My shoulders are aching,
   my eyes feel like they've got grit in them.
My legs have turned to iron
   and I'm so hungry
   I might have to eat
   some of the presents I bought.

Christmas is nearly here, Lord,
   and I'm rather thankful.
I've spent the last however many hours
   running around trying to satisfy
   the world's idea of what Christmas is about.
Now,
   exhausted,
   I wonder what the point of it all was.
Unnecessary stress

at a time of year
that's supposed to be about celebrating
the most amazing thing that ever occurred –
your birth.

We've got it all wrong, Lord.
We've dressed the season up,
    made it nice and glitzy,
    almost in an attempt to help us forget
    what it really is all about.

If we remember that, Lord,
    if we sit and think about what it really means to us,
    I doubt we'd be running around
    filling up our credit cards.
Instead,
    we'd be out in this world,
    making sure the reality of your birth,
    the incarnation of you,
    was happening each and every day
    in each and every street
    of this world.

Open our eyes, Lord,
    and help us see your birth for what it really is –
    a gift that doesn't need a credit card.

Amen.

Come again

So, Lord,
    we've celebrated your birth for 2000 years,
    or thereabouts.
We've spent years trying to work out
    the real meaning of your message
    and made plenty of mistakes along the way.
We've discussed your teachings,
    prayed to you,
    put our hope in all that you are,
    but there's just one thing that's bothering me –
    are you ever coming back?

I've heard rumours of the second coming,
    people saying when it'll happen,
    how it'll happen.
I'm a bit confused about the whole thing really.
It sounds both scary
    and amazing,
    possible
    and impossible.

A bit like your birth, I guess.
I wonder sometimes
    if your birth has become nothing more
    than a fairytale,
    a legend.
Something we tell our children

to make them feel safe.
The reality of it
    and the reality of you and your life
    have been sifted out carefully over the years
    to make the story
    nice
    and
    safe.

Which is possibly the exact opposite
    of what you were about.
Your birth wasn't one into safety.
Your life wasn't one about feeling secure,
    avoiding risk.
    and your promises for tomorrow
    have absolutely nothing to do
    with us sitting down
    and relaxing
    believing everything's going to be all right.

Which is why I ask
    when you're coming back.
We need you, Lord,
    and this world is, I think,
    forgetting your promise
    of your return.
It's getting cosy in its own bed,
    happy and blind
    from everything you told
    so long ago.

And this Christmas,
   like so many other Christmases,
   is just another step along the road
   away from what really happened,
   what it was really about.

Wake us, Lord,
   keep us alert.
Your promise of tomorrow
   isn't about us doing nothing,
   but about us doing everything
   to make sure that when you do finally arrive
   everything that had to be done
   has been done
   and all that is left
   is for you to arrive
   in glory.

Amen.

Nearly over

It's nearly over, Lord.
The food's been eaten,
   the presents unwrapped,
   everyone either gone to bed
   or making their way there.

It's been a great day.
Lots of fun,
   lots of laughter
   and love.
Hard to believe it's over so quickly.

Now there's tomorrow to think about again.
Unfortunately.
A tomorrow I'd rather not see arrive.

I've spent so many days preparing for this one
   that I don't feel that ready to let it go.
I'm not sure I want the reality of my life
   to break into the fantasy of today.
Today wasn't just a celebration of your birth
   but a celebration of family,
   of friends,
   of life.
Now all that's left
   is some cold turkey
   and the thought of another year
   of uncertainty.

I'm not ungrateful, Lord,
   today's been great.
But it's a bit like an oasis in a desert.
You can't stay there for ever if you want to get
   to the other side.
Now,
   as evening draws to night,
   I know I've no choice but to step outside
   and move on again.

I don't know where I'm going, Lord.
I don't know what next year is for.
I suddenly feel a bit lost,
   a bit confused.

Today of all days
   I should feel safer,
   more secure in what you're about.
But I don't.
In some ways
   your birth and being reminded of it,
   disturbs me,
   makes me unsteady.
It gives me no option
   but to look at my life
   to examine it,
   work out what it's about,
   what it's for,
   its purpose.

It's questions like this, Lord,
    that I didn't expect at Christmas.
But what else can I expect?
Your birth was unusual,
    it challenged the norm.
Why should it be any different now?
Even dressed up as it is
    in nativity plays
    it is still an event
    that makes me stop and think.

Lord,
    as I head off to bed,
    from this day into the next,
    stay with me.
I'm leaving the safety of Christmas,
    of being surrounded by friends and family,
    to walk out into the world once more.
    and it's scary,
    because I want every footstep I take
    to mean something,
    and take me closer to you.

Walk with me, Lord,
    on this path I've yet to tread.

Amen.

Distorted words

You changed the world, Lord.
One birth in the back of beyond
  and the world was never the same again.
Or so we'd like to believe.

It's amazing how well your words
  have become distorted.
How easily your teachings
  have been used for persecution.
You came to liberate us
  from ourselves,
  from each other,
  and all we've managed to do
  is tangle ourselves up even more,
  weigh ourselves down with chains,
  become trapped.

How can words of freedom, of justice,
  lead to imprisonment and injustice?
It just doesn't make sense.
  but then most of the time
  we don't make much sense.

We love the ideal of working together,
  loving one another,
  but the reality of that
  and the work required
  doesn't fit in with our agenda.

We want power
  not a life revolving around
  helping others.
We want money,
  not spiritual wealth.
But perhaps that is the biggest problem:
  we want, rather than give.

Christmas, Lord,
  is all about giving.
You were given to us
  to show us the real way to live.
Somehow we need to relearn that lesson.
We need to sit in awe of your life,
  what it meant from the moment it began,
  and relive it every day
  in our own lives.

This Christmas, Lord,
  give us the courage
  to give of ourselves
  to each other,
  rather than to take
  what we need.
Help us to rediscover
  the beauty of your message
  and to each day do our all
  to love each other
  as we love ourselves.

Amen.

Memories

Lord,
   when Christmas arrives,
   I always find myself
   putting on some rose-tinted glasses
   and drifting back a few years.
A lot of the time
   it's a case of,
   'Oh, if only it was like that now.'
But this time,
   it's not.

I want to sit here
   and just briefly
   bathe in my memories.
I want to close my eyes
   and relive what Christmas was like
   when I was younger.

The expectancy of Christmas Eve,
   with all the presents under the tree.
The excitement I'd feel,
   waking early on Christmas morning.
The fun of the day,
   as the floor became a sea
   of wrapping paper
   and pine needles.
The smell of the food from the kitchen,

the sound of the crackers,
the afternoon of games
and Christmas cake.

Sometimes,
   it's easy to wallow in despair
   and think that everything's gone wrong
   and that there's nothing we can do about it.
We weep and moan about how bad everything is,
   how everything was,
   how everything should be.

It's not healthy, Lord.
Looking back
   shouldn't make us see today as something worse,
   but as another reason to get up,
   make something of the day,
   and create another memory
   worthy of tomorrow.

I want all of my memories to count, Lord,
   like these ones of Christmas I remember so well.
I want to be able to look back
   and think,
      'Yes, I lived!'

Life isn't easy
   and it was never meant to be.
But that doesn't mean it's awful
   or bound to get worse.

Life is wonderful
   and my memories of the life I've had so far
   are amazing.
They make me smile
   and laugh
   and weep
   and think
   and giggle . . .

On this day in the Christmas season, Lord,
   I thank you
   for my memories.

Amen.